FoKAL

Federation of Kentucky Academic Libraries

Innovation in FoKAL Member Institutions

FoKAL Summit 2012

Edited by:
Paul Allen Tippey & Robert A. Danielson

ISBN: 9780914368977

Innovation in FoKAL Member Institutions edited by Paul Allen Tippey and Robert A. Danielson. First Fruits Press, © 2012

Digital version at http://place.asburyseminary.edu/firstfruitsbooks/3/

For all other uses, contact:
First Fruits Press
B.L. Fisher Library Asbury Theological Seminary 204 N. Lexington Ave. Wilmore, KY 40390 http://place.asburyseminary.edu/firstfruits

FoKAL Summit (2012 : Carrollton, Ky.)
    Innovations in FoKAL Member Institutions / edited by Paul Allen Tippey and
        Robert A. Danielson
    Wilmore, Ky. : First Fruits Press, c2012. 77 p. Reports submitted by member
        libraries of the Federation of Kentucky Academic Libraries concerning
        innovations implemented in the 2011-12 academic year, plus a description of
        initiatives planned for the coming academic year.
    ISBN: 9780914368977 (pbk.)
    1. Academic libraries—Aims and objectives—Kentucky. 2. Academic libraries—
        Information technology—Kentucky. 3. Academic libraries— Kentucky. I. Title.
        II. Tippey, Paul Allen. III. Danielson, Robert A., 1969- IV. Federation of
        Kentucky Academic Libraries.
    Z732.K37 F43 2012

Design by Haley Hill

asburyseminary.edu
800.2ASBURY
204 North Lexington Avenue
Wilmore, Kentucky 40390

First Fruits
THE ACADEMIC OPEN PRESS OF ASBURY SEMINARY

Table of Contents

Institution:
Asbury Theological Seminary, Wilmore, KY

Reporter:
Paul A. Tippey, Director of Library Services

Innovations (achieved or planned):

One of the major innovations in 2011-2012 was to convert existing space into a new digitization room located on the first floor of the library. One of the walls is glass to allow library users to view scanners in progress. The room houses the new Kabis III scanner, one of the best available, which was a generous gift from Robert and Joyce Buckman. The Kabis III scanner can process more than 2,900 pages an hour and features a special book cradle that is specifically designed to protect rare and fragile materials. The B. L. Fisher Library offers ePLACE, a digital repository that currently presents five unique collections: ATS eCommons, TREN dissertation, First Fruits Press, Partnerships, and Special Collections. The goals of the repository are to preserve Asbury Theological Seminary history, present an online space for scholarly communication, make academic material available to scholars worldwide, and share unique and valuable resources that would not otherwise be available for research. Visit ePLACE at place.asburyseminary.edu

The second major innovation in 2011-2012 was that of international collaboration. In April, the B.L. Fisher Library welcomed our first recipient of the International Librarian Fellowship. This year, a cooperative initiative between the American Theological Library Association and the Asbury Theological Seminary Library allowed a librarian from India to visit and work here for two months. Mr. Ch. Prasada Rao, the assistant librarian from the South Asia Institute of Advanced Christian Studies, was the Library's first guest. During his two months stay, Mr. Rao rotated among the different library departments, concentrating on archives. The overall aim of the fellowship is to offer a space to share experiences and deepen both of our understandings of library services. We hope the visit will be foundation for many more collaborative learning opportunities.

In late April, the Library Director and the Acquisitions staff member participated in a journey to research and develop how the library at Asbury Theological Seminary can partner with other libraries around the world. This first trip focused on Nigeria, Kenya, and Uganda. Partnering personally or electronically with librarians in other countries affords avenues of mutually beneficial resource sharing and professional advancement. This opportunity was first talked about in the fall of 2010, when the leadership of the seminary offered the possibility of travel to our partner institutions for library collaboration. In short, this trip has created a collegial relationship with the leadership of each of these institutions and their libraries. As each of you know, library work is continuous and ever changing in a technological age. This was truly an awesome opportunity to be able to take the skills and tools of librarianship and collaborate with other libraries across the world.

Another innovation for 2011-2012 was the creation of the Media Commons on the first floor. This office is a merger of Academic Production and Production Services. Media Commons producers are responsible for all classroom and event production that is not produced for marketing outside of the Seminary community. For example, Media

Commons maintains, supports and runs distance learning classrooms and provides production support for conferences and the President's Retreat. Additionally, the B. L. Fisher Library has introduced a library liaison program for the faculty. Every school has been assigned a library liaison, a library staff member whose educational background, interests and professional experience reflect the work of the department. The liaison does not replace, but augments the existing services of the Faculty Instructional Commons by bringing the library to the faculty.

Within the next two years, the library plans to hire another professional, and the focus of this new position will be to extend our current model of an Information Commons by adding a Learning Commons to academic support services, specifically providing writing and tutoring support and instructional design and to help faculty integrate information literacy skills within online and face-to-face courses.

Institution:
Asbury University, Wilmore, KY

Reporter:
Morgan Tracy, Director of Library Services

Innovations (achieved or planned):

One of the major planned innovations in the summer of
2012 is to convert the university's main computer lab,
currently an enclosed space located on the lower level of
the library, into a computer classroom, and distribute 35
of the computers that were in the lab to other spots
within the library. Presently there are times when the
library is open and the lab is not, which often leaves
students frustrated, and in this new arrangement all of
the student use computers would be available whenever
the library is open. Approximately half of the computers
will be in an area close to the library's service desks, while
the other half will be clustered in pods of 3-4 at other
spots. To make room for the computers near the service
desks, we are planning to weed most of our print
periodical indexes. Library student workers at the
Circulation and Reference Desks will be trained to help
support computer usage questions, and student workers
from IT will also be available during peak usage times.

Another major planned innovation for the summer of
2012 is to replace all of the furniture in a common area
on the lower level of the library. Presently that space has
8 heavy rectangular tables that are hardwired into the
floor and cannot be moved. Each of the 8 tables has a
fixed table lamp that blocks the ability of students in
groups to see each other diagonally across the table.
There are also 6 loveseats and sofas that are hard to move

in the area, and two fixed TVs. Our plan, to help encourage more group study and collaboration, is to replace the fixed tables with modular tables that can be configured in a number of different ways, accommodating groups from 2 to 30, and the chairs associated with the tables will also be mobile. The more plush seating will also be replaced by similarly comfortable furniture with wheels. Additionally, the two TVs will be connected to computers for students to use in-group projects, and students will be supplied with mobile keyboards. Finally, the area will have several mobile whiteboards that will double as privacy walls if groups choose to use them that way.

Within the next two years, the library plans to hire another professional librarian, and the focus of this new position will be on instructional design, to help faculty integrate information literacy skills within online and face-to-face courses. Coordinating the assessment of information literacy skill development among students will also be a key duty for this new position.

Recent innovations that the library has already achieved include:

- o Acquisition of more online resources for media, including Films on Demand for video recordings, Naxos for audio recordings, and ArtStor for images
- o Relocation of all academic support services to the library, including the campus writing and tutoring center
- o Digitization of the university's campus publications (newspapers, yearbooks, etc.) -- a project in progress

Institution:
Ashland Community and Technical College, Ashland, KY

Reporter:
Matt Onion, Director of Library Services

Innovations (achieved or planned):

At our college's fall convocation last August, our president announced that funds had been set aside for new carpeting in the main library at College Drive campus. This improvement had been a long time coming, but after listing new carpet each of the previous five years on the institution's IPRE strategic needs analysis, "New Carpet" finally reached #1 on the Top 15 list of strategic needs. In October of 2011, ACTC held its first professional development in-service day for all college faculty and staff. Divisions, departments, and programs personnel were encouraged early on to come up with their specific training and POD needs and to follow a research-based POD model created by the North Central Regional Educational Laboratory. The Library Services team took the basic NCREL framework, which included such activities as individual reflection, needs analysis, and group inquiry and ran with it. The new carpet became a learning exercise in project management and teamwork, and provided the impetus for a simple but no less significant facility redesign plan.

Over the years since its 1990/91 construction, main library or Mansbach Memorial Library has aged in terms of both its collection and furnishings. With the transfer of governing authorities from UKCCS to KCTCS in 1998/99 followed by the 2003 consolidation of the former ACC with ATC, the library became saddled with an overgrown print collection of books that no longer supported current curriculum. Additionally, the aging collection, which was heavy on the humanities and other general education courses, reflected the former community college's primary role as a transfer school to UK and other 4-year institutions of higher education. Although periodic weeding and replacement of the print collection, both circulating and reference, were initiated in 2004, these processes were periodic, not systematic. By the fall of 2011, team members were well aware of how cramped, dark (non-energy efficient fluorescent tubes), and cluttered the library had become---thus, replacement of the old carpet became the catalyst for further innovation and improvement.

Innovations that the library and college have/will have achieved as of June 8, 2012 are:

- o Overall reduction of the print collection by one-third or 15,000 volumes;
- o Elimination of 10 entire shelving units, as well as eight index and six study tables from the main reading area;
- o Consolidation of stacks area into a smaller proportion of floor space;
- o Re-siting/purposing of remaining shelf units, thus creating more open areas for study and lounging;
- o Overall reutilization of library space;
- o Total change-out of all ceiling lights to energy efficient florescent tubes;
- o Total conversion of all light switches to motion sensitive on/off ones;
- o Installation of inside locks on all library office, workroom, and classroom doors.

(NOTE: Last three innovations/improvements to library, as listed above, were part of a campus-wide upgrade of facilities.)

Innovations that the library plans to implement before the end of fall semester 2013 are:

- Free consultation with our system's retained interior design firm;
- Purchase of new chairs for small group study rooms;
- Replacement of all live potted plants with artificial ones;
- Reconfiguration and reduction of current circulation desk and counter into smaller area;
- Purchase of three I-Pads for student use with OPAC searches;
- Revisions to the library's collection development plan to include more e-book acquisitions;
- New paint on library interior walls to conform to color scheme at Technology Drive campus library;
- Installation of new office and other room number signs as part of campus-wide upgrade of College Drive facilities.

Institution:
Berea College, Berea, KY

Reporter:
Anne Chase

Innovations (achieved or planned):

On-Going (may never be done)

- o *LibGuides/CampusGuides*, an easy-to-use platform, has caught the imagination of librarians, faculty members, and even one administrator. We have the standard subject guides and orientation to library services guides. The real fun started when we posted faculty essays written to support a required first-year course, digitized and linked supporting primary materials, and added links to "learn more about..." topics mentioned in the essays. We are now providing accounts to faculty members who want to create guides or just sandbox ideas for their classes.
- o *LibAnswers* is an easy way to build a public/private knowledge database to support 24/7 reference. We want one place where anyone (including student workers) can find reliable answers to common questions regarding library policies, services, resources, etc. We're also working with the Computer Center to add answers to common technology questions. This summer, reference students are using apps such as Educreations to create short point-of-use videos to be included in the responses.
- o *BEREApedia*, a Wiki project, "seeks to establish itself as a one-stop-shop for archivally-researched

and confirmed information on some of the most popular topics and questions received in the College Archives. It endeavors to link to online content in *Berea Digital* and beyond, and to provide articles and contextual information regarding the Institution's history and campus culture."

o *Berea Digital*, on the CONTENTdm platform, is our digital project to provide easy access to archival materials including historic campus publications, photos, sound and video recordings, etc. The current priority for Berea Digital is curriculum support, so we are working with faculty members to select materials and responding to student requests for materials on specific topics.

Planned

o We are planning for the renovation of the Library main floor, with construction to begin in the next year. We are planning to have a service desk shared by Circulation and the Technology Resource Center. We are also talking about Reference and the Learning Center sharing a service point. The new main floor also will provide space for Career Development, Internships, the Scholar for Teaching & Learning, the Learning Center, the Technology Resource Center, Educational Technology, plus tutoring programs. The process of bringing together so many services into a limited space has focused us on flexible, multi-use spaces and the importance of understanding the work of other areas.

Institution:
Big Sandy Community and Technical College,
Prestonsburg, KY

Reporter:
Melissa M. Forsyth, Director

Innovations (achieved or planned):

A 5-year vision and action plan was developed for the Big
Sandy libraries in 2011. The plan focused on trends of the
evolving library as indicated by the current research in
the field. Several areas were identified to be considered
as part of this plan.

The first trending area is the concept of more staff time
helping the library users with online resources as
opposed to the processing of physical items. Library users
expect the library staff to be knowledgeable and helpful
when requesting assistance finding information. We
have now focused more on professional development for
all our staff learning how to navigate the online resources
by in-house training as well as webinars provided by
vendors. Advanced training in the use of program
specific resources will be conducted at the 3 campus
libraries by one of the librarians. In the future, librarians
and library staff will be trained in the use of apps for
journal databases that can be downloaded to handheld
devices. Also, training in the digitization of resources is
planned.

The second trend is the expansion of technical support
and the infrastructure to store, access and utilize online
resources. It is anticipated that federated searching will
be made available to our students soon as well as

increased bandwidth to improve access to online resources. At present, access to librarians online is through texting or email. In the future, interactive chat will be made available to our library users.

Another trending area is the appearance of the library in future years. A concerted effort has been made to provide an area where there is comfortable seating for collaborative learning. We received 25 new laptop computers for groups of students to view and discuss information related to their class learning. Electronic signage and kiosks will be placed in each campus library to provide users information on a timely basis. The circulation area and help desk at the Prestonsburg campus will be redesigned to direct users to library personnel for immediate assistance. As more classes are taught at the Mayo campus, a computer lab will be created to accommodate the increase in computer usage.

A fourth trending area is the engaging of the community learners. The library staff will continue to sponsor the Library Seminar Series, which brings in presentations and speakers on various topics in the spring months. New are events are being planned for Smart Money Week, Career and Technical Education Month and the Bibliophiles Reading Group.

The fifth trend considered is information literacy. Information literacy skills are vital to the success of the student now and in the future. Librarians provide instruction to the students in-group sessions and one-on-one in the use of current resource technologies and evaluation of information from all types of sources. In order to assist the librarians with this, the computer lab at Prestonsburg will be converted into a smart classroom for instruction. This instruction is crucial for all students if they are to develop cutting edge information literacy skills needed to be successful in all facets of life.

Institution:
Bluegrass Community and Technical College, Lexington,
KY

Reporter:
Charles James, Director of Library/Learning Resource
Center

Innovations (achieved or planned):

This has been an interesting and challenging year at
Bluegrass, but why should this year be any different? I
am sure the same can be said by many of my colleagues in
academic libraries across the Commonwealth. We
continue to be challenged by the diverse needs of our
students and faculty who, in our case, are spread among
three campuses in Lexington, and regional campuses in
Lawrenceburg, Danville, Winchester, a couple of small
satellite locations elsewhere, and of course online
students. Throw into the mix our "Early Middle College"
high school students on campus and our Adult Basic Ed.
students and...well, you can see where this is going. As
with most of you, our budgets have been challenging, and
the news looks bleak for relief in the next biennium.
Depressed? Not really. I believe we have done some of
our best work this past year and sought new ways to
deliver services as well as grow some important new
resources.

Recent and ongoing innovations:

Online Resources:
o   Added 26 new LibGuides, ranging from general to
    specific course offerings, copyright for educators,
    evaluating websites, local historical resources,

technology news resources, faculty guide to library instruction, citation guide and writing research papers.

- o Integrated using *Opposing Viewpoints with Critical Thinking* into a number of classes as well as specific class assignments and projects that reoccur each semester.
- o Added over 3,000 new full-text resources, both single-user and multiple simultaneous-user items, where possible, from Ebrary Perpetual Access Collection. For Nursing and our Allied Health programs, we added 50 titles from the Rittenhouse R2 Digital Library, including new editions of Brandon-Hill and Doody titles.
- o Added new collections (1,400 titles) of periodicals from Science Direct: Biological & Life Sciences and Health Sciences, Social Sciences & Humanities and Physical Sciences & Engineering.
- o Added a "Find A Website" page to the Library's web resources with links by subject areas to useful websites (*http://www.bluegrass.kctcs.edu/Library/links.aspx*)
- o Moving this upcoming fiscal year from Newsbank to Ebsco's <u>Newspaper Source.</u>

Events:
- o Continued our annual celebrations with displays and programming for Banned Book Week, Native American History Month, and Black History Month. For National Poetry Month we used our new large digital monitors to run PowerPoint shows of some of our book covers with selections of poems, supplemented with works by our faculty.

- Hosted a reception and reading of selections from Pickering's Mountain, a new book by Joseph G. Anthony, BCTC English faculty.
- Hosted a "Record Album Covers" art show of albums from the 1960's through the 1990's including additional covers in a PowerPoint show on our large digital displays, and hosted a public reception with 1960's-1990's pictures of some of our faculty.
- Created a digital exhibition of "Art of the Pop-up Book" from the extensive collection of one of our librarians.

Renovations:
- Implemented a new print management system as part of a college initiative that allows students to use their printing accounts to print with options such as color, two-sided, and a secure print job that can be released at any public printer at any BCTC
- We replaced all table and carrel chairs in the library.
- Replacing all library carpeting during two weeks following Memorial Day.
- Added two very large digital monitors to the Cooper Campus Library and one at each regional site that are addressable and allow programming such as displays of the Tutoring Center, Writing Center, and Library hours, as well as any PowerPoint materials we create, such as our digital exhibitions.
- BCTC Library will have an additional facility in the first building being built at the Lexington Newtown Pike Campus. This will be the first building of our College's projected new main

campus. The 20-year master plan for the campus calls for 14 to 17 buildings on the campus after completion. Planning for the new learning resource center was completed this year, construction has begun, and classes are expected to start at the site in January 2013.

Human Resources:

o A replacement for our open FT-Temp Librarian position was recently filled by Jennifer Link, who has taught college ESL classes, has extensive public and academic library experience and brings excellent skills to our public services area.

o Due to budget constraints, and after interviewing candidates and preparing to make an offer, the College had to put on hold our recent search for the replacement of our Circulation Manager position. It is our hope in the library to hire during this next fiscal year.

o Personnel of our library have been very active within the profession this year. Some of the highlights include: President of the Kentucky Library Assoc.; Chair of KCTCS Library Circulation Committee, KCTCS Senate Advisory Committee on Promotion, SACS Off-Site Review Committee; Treasurer of Kentucky Library Association; Academic Library Section; Chair of American Library Association NMRT Online Discussion Committee; Chair of the Federation of Kentucky Academic Libraries (FoKAL) Advocacy Committee; Chair of Arts in Focus Literary Arts Subcommittee managing the publication of BCTC's literary journal; Chair of KCTCS Catalogers' Group, preparing presentations for summer workshops on interlibrary loan and cataloging issues for KCTCS catalogers and ILL staff; and library personnel aided KCTCS System Librarian with doctorial dissertation research that was, in part, a case study examining library leadership within the college.

- Library personnel at our Leestown Campus hosted a career night for our Early Childhood Education degree program, which included current students within the program interacting with a successful past graduate who talked about what they must do to prepare for the workplace, different certification tests, and what she looks for when interviewing and hiring credentialed personnel.
- To address, in part, the drop in our faculty's use of our in-class library instruction sessions, our Instructional Services Librarian established a regular schedule of hours in our Cooper Campus Tutoring and Writing Center to assist students with specific research needs. An advantage for us was that the tutors also took advantage of the services so that they could better answer questions and assist in finding the resources that we provide.

Not unlike last year, things do not look particularly rosey going into the new academic year with less staffing, tighter budgets, and growing needs from our faculty and students. Looking at what we have managed to accomplish this year however, I am convinced that we will be all right and just maybe have many new highlights to list next year.

Institution:
Bowling Green Technical College, Bowling Green, KY

Reporter:
Janice Gabbard, Director of Library and Information
Technology

Innovations (achieved or planned):

Instruction

The BGTC Library collaborates with faculty in the
Business Division to integrate two library units into
CIT105 Introduction to Computers classes. The *Website
Evaluation* and *Introduction to Research using Library
Databases* units are presented during two separate class
times. Students work in assigned groups and research
their topics using the library databases during the
Library Database unit. The groups continue to work
together during the semester, eventually presenting their
research to the class in a PowerPoint presentation.

Approximately 50 sessions were taught each semester,
working with approximately 25 different CIT105 classes.
Student response has been positive. The library team
meets with the CIT105 faculty team annually to review
the student satisfaction survey results and student
learning outcomes.

The library team plans to create LibGuides pages for the
learning units this summer to provide easy access to the
materials for the students for future research needs.

KCTCS General Education Competencies Met

Communicate Effectively
1. *Demonstrate information processing through basic computer skills.*

Think Critically
1. *Demonstrate problem solving through interpreting, analyzing, summarizing, and/or integrating a variety of materials.*

Learn Independently
1. *Use appropriate search strategies and resources to find, evaluate, and use information.*

Information Literacy Outcomes Met

Topic and Search Strategy Formulation

Technology

This year the Library and Information Technology Team has explored the implementation and support of mobile devices at the college. Identification of useful apps, device-specific challenges, data security, and best practices has been the focus. The findings will be published as an FAQ page in LibGuides.

Institution:
Brescia University, Owensboro, KY

Reporter:
Sr. Judith N. Riney, Director of Library Services

Innovations (achieved or planned):

In an effort to advertise, excite, and gain feedback from the Brescia community- at- large about library services, a project was adopted in the fall called "7 Days to Have Your Say". Posters were created using faculty, staff and students posing in humorous form to advertise the event. Emails were sent, and an article was published in the weekly student newspaper to alert the campus of the project. A weeklong email chat service, todaysmeet.com, was used to facilitate questions about various topics of library services and resources and faculty, staff, administration, and students corresponded with one another through this Internet site. Along with the online chat a number of focus groups consisting of faculty, staff and students were held as part of this project.

One of the most useful additions to the library resources was the purchase and implementation of *LibGuides*. A Hart Grant was obtained during the summer of 2011 to work with an interested faculty from each of the academic divisions to assist faculty with incorporating course syllabi with *LibGuides* to provide relevant library links for specific courses. This workshop was a success and throughout the year the *LibGuides* were used quite successfully among students and faculty.

Since texting is the culture of the day among students, the library created a texting service so students could contact the library staff using smart phones to request assistance in using library resources. This service will be expanded during the next fiscal year with the addition of *LibAnswers* to increase library support.

A library open house was held in the spring semester for the Brescia community to honor all tenured faculty. Books that had special meaning for tenured faculty were displayed and bookplates were attached to each book to commemorate the faculty's achievements.

The library signed on to be a host site in the first ever international World Book Night, April 23. Our library was one of 600 libraries in the U.S. participating in the half million book give away in 6,000 towns and cities to promote reading and love of books. The library staff hosted a reception for all book givers and distributed books to be donated. This event was a huge success and the library will volunteer to serve as a book distributor again next year.

Additional new online services offered during 2011-2012: *Historic Documents, Gale Virtual Reference Database*

Institution:
Clear Creek Baptist Bible College, Pineville, KY

Reporter:
Marge Cummings, Director of Library Services

Innovations (achieved or planned):

One of the innovations planned for the library this summer is a weeding of the Devotional/Christian Living collection before doing inventory of that section. Another major weeding project is being performed on the VHS collection, replacing the frequently circulating titles with DVDs when possible and finding alternate titles when an exact replacement cannot be located.

Computer Services has been working with our ISP to improve services. The new fiber optic Internet connection is now located in an upstairs room of the library – a more central location, between the classroom building and the administrative offices. At 10 MB, access is much faster.

The summer story hour will begin June 7th for campus children and those attending the Child Development Center.

The college is experiencing some administrative personnel changes. The Computer Services Director is leaving to begin full-time ministry and his assistant has been named Dean of Administrative Affairs. The new Computer Services Director will be coming to campus in June.

Institution:
Frontier Nursing University, Hyden, KY

Reporter:
Billie Anne Gebb, Director of Library Services

Innovations (achieved or planned):

Recent innovations achieved at our library include using
OCLC's CONTENTdm to archive the written portion of
our Doctor of Nursing Practice (DNP) students' capstone
projects. We have also begun offering drop-in webinars
for advanced searching skills (using the institutional
access to Blackboard Collaborate). These sessions have
been so well received that they have led to more
opportunities to integrate library instruction into existing
coursework. At the beginning of 2012 we implemented
Clio for interlibrary loan processing, which has
automated much of our process and eliminated a lot of
paper! Our library has also been very successful at
achieving innovations in mobile resources, supporting
students and faculty with download and usage
information.

Innovations planned for the upcoming year include
renovating our physical library space to remove most
print materials and make the space more conducive for
work and collaboration by adding computers, docking
stations, mobile device chargers, and comfortable
seating. We plan to renovate our online space as well by
revising the library website, perhaps using LibGuides for
the entire site. We also have the opportunity to integrate
our existing library tutorial into a course required for all
students. It will be interesting see outcomes for this new
project. We will continue working with CONTENTdm to

create a digital archive of historical photos from the Frontier Nursing Service and early days of our school. We also hope to add more multimedia to our collection, and continue supporting mobile resources with a LibGuide devoted to those resources and a mobile friendly library website.

Institution:
Gateway Community & Technical College, Covington, KY

Reporter:
Charlene McGrath, Director Library and Information Services

Innovations (achieved or planned):

The most innovative feature of the GCTC library is that we do not have a circulating collection. Students, faculty and staff may use Northern Kentucky University library for circulation services and interlibrary loans as well as check out books from the regional public libraries.

Sixth District School- Reading partners program as part of the B.E.S.T. Program. Staff members volunteer for one-on-one reading enrichment with elementary school students at the Sixth District School in Covington.

Embedded Librarians-, an embedded librarian project began in 15 online classes. Library staff has access to the class via Blackboard, enabling them to provide information literacy training and reference assistance to online students. Through posted tutorials, quizzes, and discussion board posts, library staff is able to meet the library research needs of distance education students. Enrollment in online classes has risen and, as more courses have online components, the GCTC library anticipates a continued expansion of the embedded librarian program.

Tutorials- The library developed 17 online tutorial modules using Camtasia Studio software. The tutorials are short (two – three minutes in length) and range from general GCTC library information to information literacy concepts and specific assignment assistance. Tutorials are located in LibGuides.

LibGuides- a content management system was added September 2011 in order to upgrade GCTC's research guides and promote library resources. LibGuides also provides the means to integrate multimedia content into library services, creating a more interactive, user-friendly service.

LibAnswers-was added in September 2011 to provide ask-a-librarian functions when staff is not on duty. Questions can be submitted by chat, telephone, or email. Questions and answers are archived and available on the site.

eBooks and Databases- collection of eBooks has increased by 350%. Four new databases have been purchased during 2011-2012, all at the request of the faculty.

Tablets- will be purchased during the summer for each library to provide additional access to GCTC resources.

Institution:
Hazard Community and Technical College, Hazard, KY

Reporter:
Cathy Branson, Director of Library Services

Innovations (achieved or planned):

Library locations at Hazard Community and Technical College underwent renovations in the summer and fall of 2011. Paint, new carpeting and furniture were purchased to improve appearance and create flexible seating configurations. A new circulation desk was purchased for the Lees College Campus Library. A classroom/computer lab was created in a space previously devoted to the library's collection of children's books. The computer lab located in the Stephens Library was updated with new tables and all new PCs. Shelving was relocated to promote the Stephens Library collection of fiction and graphic novels.

The installation of a large flat screen television in the Lees College Campus Library's study area provided an additional area for viewing audiovisuals and gaming. At the Stephens Library location several large furniture items were relocated to Leslie County in preparation of opening an additional resource space at the Kentucky School of Bluegrass and Traditional Music in 2012-13.

A collaborative program was held at the Knott County Public Library promoting the career and resume resources of HCTC.

2013 plans include the final preparations for opening the Leslie County site. This space will house an archival collection of Bluegrass Music audiovisuals, eReaders and resources/equipment in support of this unique program. An NEH grant (America's Music) was submitted in spring of 2012. If awarded grant funding, a series of film and musical performances will be hosted in the HCTC service area. Students and faculty of HCTC/ KSBTM will be among the featured performers. Local public libraries supported HCTC Libraries' grant application. Programming and/or other collaboration at these library locations will be part of the NEH project plan.

Digitization of the oral history collection of the Lees College Campus will continue with purchasing of preservation materials and adequate long-term storage of the physical collection. Additional purchases will include software to facilitate digitization.

2013
- o Collection development and weeding
- o Reconfiguration of furniture layout at the Stephens Library.
- o Additional furniture purchases for the Leslie County site
- o Adoption/purchase of additional software/equipment/resources to support online students

Institution:
Hopkinsville Community College, Hopkinsville, KY

Reporter:
Cynthia Atkins, Director of Library Services

Innovations (achieved or planned):

The College's quality enhancement plan, which focuses on reading, will commence in fall 2012. In a support function, the HCC Library has begun collecting graphic novels, science fiction/fantasy literature, and both fiction and non-fiction best sellers.

A project to weed all vhs-format videotapes is nearing completion. Films on Demand has been added to the Library database holdings, and replacement DVDs are being ordered when available. This has been a cooperative effort between the teaching faculty and the library staff.

The professional staff offered a Choose Privacy session for students in conjunction with ALA's Choose Privacy Week. We hope to have an event each year to encourage responsible use of personal information. We also did our annual display during Banned Book Week.

After successfully writing a grant and being selected as one of the initial 25 host libraries in the U.S., the HCC Library staff welcomed the Lincoln: The Constitution and the Civil War exhibit to campus in late September. Prior to its arrival, the College hosted an in-service training for area teachers taught by a Constitution Center representative. During its six-week stay, the Library staff partnered with several community groups to offer programs related to the exhibit.

Following a successful pilot, the online version of the library instruction/information literacy unit was rolled out to distance learners enrolled in English 101 classes.

A full-time position was added. This individual has been charged with overseeing and enhancing the formal instruction/information literacy program.

Two new databases, Learning Express and Nursing Digital Library were acquired. In July, Lib Guides will be picked up as well.

Planning for a study room/lounge is in the early formative stage at this time.

Institution:
Jefferson Community and Technical College, Louisville, KY

Reporter:
Sheree Huber Williams, Director of Library Services

Innovations (achieved or planned):

o   Offering instruction in workshop format. We offer a schedule of workshops lasting 30-45 minutes on many of the basic information literacy topics including introduction to the library, MLA and APA citations, using e-books, and searching databases. This gives faculty an option for providing information literacy instruction for students that doesn't require use of class time and provides students with an opportunity to attend workshops matching their needs.

o   Re-designed programming space. We moved our programming and workshops into an open space near the front entrance of the library. It is easily accessible to students just walking by allowing us to draw in students who otherwise might not have attended.

o   Collaborative workspace. We are designating space for students to work collaboratively and furnishing to accommodate group work. Each table has a flat panel monitor and a switch that allows connection of multiple laptops to the flat panel. We have a couple of mobile whiteboards that can be moved between stations.

o   Flexible instructional space at the Technical Campus Library. This small library was set up in a way that made it difficult to accommodate formal instruction to classes. The space is being re-worked and an instructor's computer and projector are being installed. Steelcase Node chairs are being purchased which can be configured into a more formal arrangement for instruction, into clusters for small group work, or moved apart for individual study.

o Technology "sandbox." We have begun to purchase limited quantities of different devices allowing faculty, staff and students to experiment and perhaps "try before you buy." Our budget is small but we have some GPS units, a few Kindles, some iPods and a couple of iPads.

o Chalkboard wall. Although low-tech this has actually been very popular. We painted a wall just inside the library entrance with chalkboard paint and use it to post the "Word of the Week" where we feature a word, provide the definition and use it in a sentence. We have also used the wall to advertise programming and post other information.

o LCD board to advertise workshops and programming. We use an LCD board that lights up and changes color to advertise daily programming and workshops.

Using social media. We use our Facebook page to promote library programming, resources and workshops and connect with out students, faculty and staff. We have also linked to some very brief humorous "Word of the Week" videos we created using Xtranormal.

Institution:
Kentucky Christian University, Grayson, KY

Reporter:
Naulayne Enders, Director of Young Library

Innovations (achieved or planned):

Tutoring Center: In the Fall of 2011, the tutoring center at Kentucky Christian University moved into the library building from a classroom building. This has been a highly successful venture. The tutoring center is available to help students in a centralized location that was already a gathering and work place. It also allows the tutoring center staff to bring students to library employees in order to help them acquire information and resources. The students can then return to the tutoring center to acquire help in using those resources. There has been a significant increase in user statistics for both the library and the tutoring center.

Space Repurposing: Adding the tutoring center has led to a re-evaluation of how space is being utilized in the library. Our bound periodical room is in the process of being weeded to allow for more space for the tutoring center. Also, areas that have previously been used as storage areas are being cleared and evaluated for use as quiet study areas and group study rooms.

Speaker Series: Young Library began promoting the idea of on campus speakers in the library in the spring of 2011. Up until this point, there had been no presentations in the library for several years. Through our Public Services librarian several departments were approached for collaboration. Our History department, our Bible and Ministry Department, and our English department have provided speakers. The library provides advertising materials and light refreshments. This partnership has yielded a great turnout for these events.

Facebook/ Social Media Policy: During the summer of 2011, the library developed a Facebook page. This page was designed to provide information and reading encouragement to both on campus and off-campus patrons. In order to be consistent with content and postings, the library developed a social media policy, the first on Kentucky Christian University's campus.

Faculty Training Grant: The library received a Faculty Enrichment in Library Resources Grant through the Appalachian College Association. This grant allowed the library to provide instruction on library resources to campus faculty. Over 80% of the faculty participated in this optional professional development opportunity and every department on campus was represented. Instruction was provided on new technologies for instruction and research. Discussions were held with the faculty on how to incorporate the new technologies.

Archival collection: The changing of new staff brought to the library a librarian with archival experience. This has allowed us to begin developing an official archival collection. This will allow the library to have better use of its storage space and will improve university-wide access to materials.

Institution:
Kentucky State University, Frankfort, KY

Reporter:
Sheila A. Stuckey, Director of Libraries

Innovations: Transforming Library Spaces

Kentucky State University, Paul G. Blazer Library has collaborated with Developmental Education and the Academic Center for Excellence (ACE) to create a state of the art, smart classroom to support the University's "Academics With Attitude: Building the Foundation for Student Success" (AWA) project, a focused five-year Quality Enhancement Plan for academically at-risk students. The classroom and lab is outfitted with state-of-the-art equipment, including 20 PCs, a SMART Board interactive whiteboard, projector and instructor podium, and new tables and chairs. The library space was previously used as a media classroom for instruction, workshops and community events. The new classroom is currently used for instruction, tutoring, mentoring, and group study. It is staffed with peer academic support staff and an instructional counselor. Blazer Library faculty and staff provide assistance and instruction to individual students and entire classes as requested by faculty for course assignment and projects. The Library also uses the space for its regular library instruction classes.

The Library has an extended hour study room accessible from the front entrance of the Library. This space is available to students for studying and is used most often after the Library is closed. The room is also used for library programming and occasionally for instruction.

The future plan is to update this space with comfortable seating, oval lounge and group study tables, and additional lighting. The new furniture will provide students access to a comfortable updated environment for studying and lounging.

A few years ago, a room in the Library's Periodicals area, which was once used as the microfilm room, was converted into a "Music Listening Lab" for music faculty and students to listen to music CDs from the Library's music CD collection. A new development for this space will be the relocation of the Library's music score collection from the 2nd floor stacks to shelving units in this area, for easier access for our music faculty and students.

Currently, we are implementing modest, cost effective changes and enhancements, however, in the future; it is our plan to improve the Library's physical spaces and services to best address the learning and research needs of our students, faculty and staff. In the next few years, we plan to hire a consultant to assist us in creating a long-term plan for a major facility upgrade and renovation.

Institution:
Louisville Presbyterian Theological Seminary, Louisville, KY

Reporter:
Carolyn Cardwell, Instructional Technology Administrator

Innovations (achieved or planned):

An alumnus, the Rev. David Sharp, donated a collection of religious art to the seminary, and the library was charged with organizing and maintaining the collection. We wanted a way to make the art available to faculty, students, and other researchers without having to circulate the actual collection, much of which is on display around campus.

The Head of Public Services gathered information about the artists and their works, the former Head of Technical Services identified OCLC's CONTENTdm as a free resource for organizing and displaying digitized items, and the Instructional Technology Administrator set up the CONTENTdm site, entered the metadata, and uploaded the images. Fine-tuning of the site is on going.

Now the Sharp Art Collection is discoverable through WorldCat, directly findable under its own URL (http://cdm16132.contentdm.oclc.org/cdm), and the images are viewable by anyone.

We plan to add other donated art to the site as time allows.

Institution:
Madisonville Community College, Madisonville, KY

Reporter:
Cherry Berges, Director of Library Services

Innovations (achieved or planned):

Professional Development:
- o Two daylong library staff retreats are held each year, one in June and one in December. At each, we spend half the day in updating and the other half focusing on a specific topic or topics, which we will be incorporating during the coming months. We often have experts come present to us and try to make it an active learning opportunity for all staff and librarians, no matter what their responsibilities.
- o Increased funds and opportunities for staff, as well as librarians, to participate in online training related to their functions and/or to attend conferences as possible.
- o Librarians plan to visit several libraries during fy12/13, particularly those that are implementing variations of Learning Commons.

Information Literacy Instruction
- o During the past year, we have incorporated use of Quizdom clickers into face-to-face info lit instruction as a means of assessment.
- o We acquired and began building and using LibGuides for independent learners and as a means of providing instruction to online classes (with embedded quizzes)

- o Improving information literacy instruction is under continuous revision from year-to-year, as we refine the tools. We use hands-on instruction in our laptop lab.

Collection
- o We anticipate radical weeding in the reference collection, with a corresponding shift to increased online resources.
- o Making sufficient time for radical weeding in Q-Zs is on our agenda for Su'12/F'12 prior to major shelf-shifting.

Planning
- o MCC has developed a plan for expansion of the Muhlenberg Campus. A part of this includes a space for library resources, services, and instruction. Our library plan will be competed this summer. We have added a faculty member who will be working to support the library mission part-time at that location.

Services
- o We have several Nook and Nook Colors that we circulate.
- o The Library Committee initiated a series of student discussion groups led by members of the teaching faculty (rotating among divisions) and held here in the library. We acquired several copies to make available to students for reading. An English instructor led *The Hunger Games Trilogy*. A history teacher led discussion of *The Help*. And a biology faculty member is deciding what to begin with in the fall semester.

Institution:
Maysville Community and Technical College Library,
Maysville, KY

Reporter:
Sonja R. Eads

Innovations (achieved or planned):

As students are learning in different ways in the
classroom, so are they studying in different ways. Over
the last 10 – 15 years we have seen how students have
shifted from looking for research materials from the print
to non-print collections. Students are studying more in
small groups and are gathering in quiet places (even if
they aren't so quiet!) to collaborate. Students use the
Internet to find resources for assignments. Students are
asking for more help with technology as well.

The MCTC library has been adding more e-books,
electronic databases, and providing computer lab
assistance for over fifteen years. Last year, after
assessing library surveys, computer lab report logs, focus
groups and observations, we decided the best way to
provide the resources, services and space students need
was to move toward a learning commons concept.
Providing the space in the way students seem to want to
use the library was the major focus. Our first step was to
consult with a professional design team. We contacted
CG Concepts, a design company used by KCTCS, to assess
our current space at each of our three campus libraries.
Next was securing funding, which the library requested
and was approved by college leadership the majority from
nonrecurring funds. Since the library is not getting a new
space, we really had to focus on what space we have and

how to make that space work. Each campus library is different and the amount of space varies greatly. The Maysville campus is the biggest space and the location where more students use the library.

We worked with the Maysville campus first to weed at least a third of the print collection. The professional librarians assessed everything from VHS to Reference to Oversize and all of the regular stacks. Removing books from the library was not a popular topic, especially among some of the faculty. What to do with the discards became very controversial. We contacted Better World Books and they graciously took everything we wanted to send them.

The library staff removed books based on age, last date of use, subject matter and physical condition. Once we got over the initial shock of taking books off the shelf forever, it became rather therapeutic! A distinct pattern began emerging. We noticed that for a great majority, books had not circulated after 1996. That was when we set up the computer lab and provided Internet access to students. Some subject areas were no longer valid because they were so outdated they were irrelevant to the current curriculum. This also provided the librarians with an opportunity to select new titles for purchase to update and revise subject areas. For example, I wiped out Latin America. Everything on the shelf was so old I was embarrassed to have anyone ask for help in that history section! When we assessed the literature collection, some copies of classics were in such a deteriorating shape, we withdrew and decided not to replace them after checking to see if they were in our e-book collections or available from a free/open source like Project Gutenberg. Even though we have been building up our electronic books collections, we have not pushed those to our students to use. Let's face it; looking at a book on the computer is very different than holding a book in hand and thumbing through the pages. If it is not pleasure reading or an article from a reference book in an electronic database, reading on the computer is awkward.

This is our next challenge, to provide better ways of accessing the 57,000 plus e-books in our collection. We purchased three Kindle 2s (one for each of our libraries), but have only circulated them to faculty. Starting this year, we will begin circulating them to students and purchasing more Kindle titles. We just purchased the latest Kindle Fire devise. We are also looking at providing other devises, such as iPads or smart tablets, to circulate to students this coming year.

At the Rowan and Licking Valley campuses we did very little weeding because they are newer libraries and the collections are not as outdated. We have reconsidered our Reference collections at each campus and decided that the reference books might be more useful if they circulated. We are in the process of decommissioning our reference collections to a chosen few, such as a basic encyclopedia, a copy of the style manuals, or a desktop dictionary. With our online reference e-books, and of course anything from the Internet, the traditional reference collections have been neglected. We hope that this will prove to be a positive move for students who may go to the circulating books and pass the things they can't check out.

The library has a small set of funds for part-time assistance. We are trying to provide more I.T. support in a part-time capacity until we can demonstrate the need for a full time position. We hope that we can also provide literacy help for our developmental education courses but do not have a full-blown plan for that as yet.

Our goal is to transform the libraries to a Learning Commons environment. The first phase is looking at existing space and how to convert those areas into a more inviting and welcoming place. The next phase will be implementation of changing the space along with reviewing our services and support. Hopefully, next year, we can report our progress.

Institution:
Morehead State University, Morehead, KY

Reporter:
Ray Bailey and David Gregory

Innovations (achieved or planned):

o Creation of a library commons area with 23 computers, movable furniture, multiple screens, and whiteboards to facilitate student collaboration.
o Addition of the university Tutoring and Learning Center in the area adjacent to the commons.
o Creation of three reservable, high-tech study/collaboration rooms (two completed, one planned).
o Fifteen computer workstations added to Learning Resource Center area.
o Computer workstations added to various areas of the library for patron use.
o Addition of pay-for-print color printing capability.
o Two new Macs for patron use.
o Purchase of 30 iPads with charging/syncing cart (planned)
o Addition of a Multicultural Room designed to highlight diversity on campus.
o Collaboration with Document Services, Offices of Undergraduate Research, and the Center for Regional Engagement to provide a large-scale poster printer to the campus.
o Weeding of VHS collection (ongoing) and the addition of Films on Demand to our subscriptions.

Institution:
Owensboro Community and Technical College,
Owensboro, Kentucky

Reporter:
Donna Abell, Director of Library Services

Innovations (achieved or planned):

(Most initiatives are products of OCTC Library's strategic plan.)

Library Staff is active with community outreach

Fall in Love with Reading
An annual event is held at the OCTC Library collaborating OCTC's Women in Support of Education (WISE) group and the Imagination Library Community Advisory Panel. This is an awareness event for the Daviess County Chapter of the Dolly Parton Imagination Library program, which promotes and supports early childhood literacy.

Ready to Read program
To promote early childhood literacy, OCTC Library Staff started a reading program this year with on-campus Dar-Nek Daycare Center and local Cravens Elementary School, in which the staff visits the children there and reads books to them. There are plans for the children to visit the library for readings in the newly installed *Cornelia's Corner*, which is a small area in the OCTC Library dedicated in memory of an early childhood education faculty member, the late Dr. Cornelia Glenn.

Library, Teaching & Learning Center, and Cyber

Center --one location

In the past year, the Cyber Center became part of the OCTC Library's space, which includes seventy-five computers for students to use. It joins the Teaching and Learning Center, which has been in the Library for several years. Staff members of the Library, Cyber Center, and TLC communicate with each other on a daily basis, promoting resources and services of each department to the students. The physical arrangement and relationships between the Library, TLC, and Cyber Center have increased usage of library resources and services, and most importantly, allowed convenient and improved service to our students.

Partners with Common Reading Committee

The OCTC Library Staff works closely with the OCTC Common Reading Committee, which has created a very successful program. A different book is chosen for the common read each semester. The library creates various book and DVD displays and purchases jigsaw puzzles and posters related to the book for all three OCTC campuses. Students LOVE the puzzles. Many of the puzzles are framed and permanently placed on the library walls for viewing by all. Various events are sponsored/hosted by both Library and Common Reading Committee each semester. The 10th anniversary of the Common Reading will be in 2014, at which time we anticipate previous Common Read authors to revisit our campus. Some of them include Silas House, Wendell Berry, Bobbie Ann Mason, Davis McCombs, Frank X Walker, Stephen Berry, and Sherman Alexie.

Mini workshops

The Library Staff has recently started a series of mini workshops (20 minutes in length) to promote various library resources, such as specific databases or interlibrary loan services to students. Also, workshops on topics such as financial and information literacy are presented. To promote attendance and participation during Q & A, incentives are offered. OCTC Faculty and Library Staff present the workshops.

Institution:
Southeast Kentucky Community and Technical College, Cumberland, KY

Reporter:
Warren Gray

Innovations (achieved or planned):

We have expanded the opening hours of the Harlan campus library by assigning a professional librarian to work there two additional days per week, except during summer. This has resulted in greatly increased library usage and much better, more consistent service on that campus. So far, the ABE students and academic students in night classes are the main ones being reached. Next year a major effort will be made to involve more of the daytime tech instructors and students with the library. The carpentry students are currently constructing a night book drop.

Last year, we used college grant money to purchase a limited number of Kindle and Nook e-books and readers, and we are buying more this year using regular library funds. This year's grant money has been used to buy digital camcorders for use by faculty, staff and students to record projects and events.

New ID making equipment was installed in Cumberland and Middlesboro this past year and has just been added in Whitesburg and Harlan. ID's are a way in which we serve the college as a whole, but they also serve as library cards and introduce students to the library early in their college experience.

New carpeting was installed in all campus libraries the summer before last. The Whitesburg library followed that up with a new circulation desk, other furniture, and a nice new color-coordinated look.

The Middlesboro and Harlan campuses participated in World Book Night, distributing free special editions of books selected specifically for "reluctant readers," of which we have no shortage.

We have just begun a subscription to LibGuides. Nothing much has been done yet, except that several of us have attended webinars and done a little experimenting with it. We hope to make good use of it during the summer and the coming year. We will also be looking at a possible source of online test study guides and related materials.

The Middlesboro and Whitesburg campuses plan to replace their older televisions with new flat screen models. Funds for two in Middlesboro have been obtained, and they will be mounted in the corners of the library for easy student viewing.

Institution:
Thomas More College, Crestview Hills, KY

Reporter:
Jim McKellogg, Library Director

Innovations (achieved or planned):

One of our planned innovations is to partner with
Student Support Services in helping at-risk students, by
assisting them in their use of library resources, through
one-on-one tutoring sessions and/or by participating in
student success workshops. This more proactive
approach to reference service and information literacy
instruction is based on the assumption that at-risk
students who are struggling in other areas of their college
experience are probably also having difficulty using
library resources to complete their assignments, but may
not be forthcoming in asking for help.

Institution:
Union College, Barbourville, KY

Reporter:
Sean Jump, Library Assistant

Innovations (achieved or planned):

There are a number of summer 2012 innovations planned for the Weeks-Townsend Memorial Library. One of the principal projects involves the digitization of videotapes in the library holdings. This will be a two-part project, which will transfer many video recordings of historical Union College events to the more functional DVD format. A related project is the weeding of the entire VHS collection, which will eliminate videotapes that are no longer of use to the library due to duplication, obsolescent information, or physical flaws.

Another major project to be undertaken is a complete inventory of the library Stacks. A portable scanner will be used by those assigned to this project to scan every book in the Stacks. The list obtained will be compared to previous inventories to produce an updated catalog for the collection with regards to item availability and status. As with the VHS project, a weeding of the Stacks will also be conducted, and this will cull unneeded extra books so that available Stacks shelf space may be maximized.

Similar weeding projects will be undertaken for the Curriculum, Reference and Government Document collections. Curriculum material, which is not up to date and therefore no longer of use to our student teachers, will be withdrawn (most likely to be placed on our Free Book shelf), while Reference items will be evaluated to determine if they are still reliable and current sources of information to our patrons. Documents that have been supplanted by more recent publications will be pulled and offered to other institutions so as to free up valuable shelf space for the continued growth of the collection.

Finally, the library recently concluded a survey of Union College students pertaining to library services, and one part of the greater Library Strategic Plan Initiative. This Initiative began with a SWOT analysis in December of 2011, and a final version of the Strategic Plan will be completed in July of 2012. This Strategic Plan will drive all library assessment for 2012 and 2013. The survey, which was implemented via SurveyMonkey, asked students for input on a wide variety of library-related issues, from which areas within the library they most enjoyed to what sorts of changes they would like to see implemented. The survey produced some valuable insights into what our student users like and do not like about the library, though we were gratified that most responses were favorable overall. The results of this survey will be taken under advisement as the library continues to evolve in an ongoing effort to better meet the needs of our student users.

Institution:
University of Kentucky Libraries, Lexington, KY

Reporter:
Terry Birdwhistell

Innovations (achieved or planned):

UK Libraries is moving to a virtualized computer environment for public computing. This move will be in place before the fall semester begins in August. Using a Citrix based solution, users will log into a virtual desktop environment with their UK credentials. Software is licensed and distributed from a central server. This virtualized environment can run on older equipment because the power for running the software applications comes from the central server. Service needs will be greatly reduced because the virtualized environment is less vulnerable to viruses and user introduced problems. As the older machines fail they can be replaced with much less expensive thin clients, thus reducing the overall cost of providing desktop computing in the library and library classrooms.

UK Libraries is developing a secure enterprise wide repository for digital content. UK Libraries is taking the technical lead on the development of this repository that meets current digital preservation standards. The repository is based on an Open Archival Information System model and utilizes micro services to perform repository functions. This repository will not only preserve all digital library content created by Kentucky libraries for the Kentucky Digital Library, but also research data sets and other digital content created to support the research enterprise.

Special Collections has brought their historic onsite exhibits into the 21st century with the addition of two iPad kiosks. The kiosks allow for the creation of enhanced context in a user friendly and interactive interface. Importantly it allows curators to add audio and moving images into traditional exhibit spaces. Additionally, the kiosks will be used for interactive Special Collections displays and information in a format that our current users demand.

OHMS: Innovation: The Louie B. Nunn Center created an open source web-based, tool called OHMS (Oral History Metadata Synchronizer) to inexpensively and efficiently enhance access to and discovery of oral histories online. The OHMS tool connects a user from a search term in a transcript or an index to the corresponding moment in the online audio or video. The Nunn Center currently has about 700 oral history interviews online utilizing the transcript synchronizing technology. The newly developed indexing module of OHMS creates a searchable online index containing a variety of descriptive fields that also connect to the corresponding moment in the audio or video interview. The interview index can be created for a fraction of the cost of verbatim transcription and can be done much more quickly. OHMS is a free and open source tool that empowers repositories to significantly enhance the ways they provide online access to oral history interviews.

Special Collections is transforming the way we utilize undergraduate and graduate assistants. In treating Special Collections as a *Learning Laboratory* we are matching students to primary source materials that fit their areas of research. The SC Learning Lab will enhance the potential for student research and make new collections available for researchers worldwide.

The Academic Affairs and Research Division of UK Libraries uses Springshare's LibAnalytics to collect data on library instruction sessions, strategic plan progress, quarterly report activities, and some public services statistics. We use LibAnswers/RefAnalytics for the rest of our public services statistics; we moved to this system in January after using LibStats for over four years. We are an early adopter of LibAnalytics and have developed a detailed form for collecting information about library instruction in particular. Collecting data in this fashion is considerably easier than collecting emails, sharing a spreadsheet, using a SurveyMonkey form, or other systems that were used in the past. Using these tools gives us a searchable database that provides many reporting and analysis options.

Institution:
University of Pikeville, Pikeville, KY

Reporter:
Karen Evans

Innovations (achieved or planned):

We are currently weeding our collection to create additional study areas on the third floor.

In the fall, the writing center and the academic assistance program (tutoring) will move under the supervision of the Library which will increase availability and visibility for those two areas. The former writing center will become a conference/media room. Students will have access to a large monitor, which can be connected to a laptop for group work, presentation equipment, so that they will have an area to practice and create presentations, and an area to watch media in small groups.

We plan to pilot a patron driven acquisitions system for the nursing and medical students in the fall with Rittenhouse.

The instruction program has expanded dramatically with 148 classes being taught during the 2011-2012 year. An additional instruction librarian is being considered.

Institution:
Western Kentucky University, Bowling Green, KY

Reporter:
Connie Foster, Interim Dean of Libraries

Innovations (achieved or planned):

- In planning stages is a redesigned Cravens 4th floor entrance and single-service point for an Information Commons with combined services for research, technology and the writing center alongside Circulation Services. We plan to provide more comfortable, flexible seating in the former Reference area. We have also opened up former "typing" rooms for 1-2 person study and have placed 81/2x11 signs at key desk areas advertising study space of various types in the library, as well as on our web site.
- Awarded for the 3rd semester the collaborative WKU Libraries and University Experience Undergraduate Research Award to a student from the main campus that prepares the best annotated bibliography and a student from the South Campus who writes the best career essay. The students are given a plaque and a $100 check for their achievements. Their content is uploaded to TopSCHOLAR, WKU's institutional repository.
- Worked with an Art Installation class to produce two art projects using discarded, withdrawn books or non-accepted gift books. One project is Flying Books to be installed on a wall on Cravens 4th floor; the second, a set of "tapestries" using book pages and beeswax to produce a translucent effect as the pieces hang in the Reference Area in Helm.

- The Library and Information Technology are blending library technology needs into a Library Systems Office with full and part-time positions, funded by Information Technology but which reside in the library. The Dean of Libraries sets priorities; the Director of Academic Technology and the Senior Library Technology Consultant implement these priorities. The existing library faculty for systems and web and emerging technologies remain part of their respective departments. We believe this hybrid arrangement to be unique and look forward to meeting many needs and creating new services.
- Designed a special "Library Jeopardy Game" to teach new classroom faculty about library services as part of the New Faculty Orientation. They had a folder of information, divided into teams, and played the game!
- Launched our first in-house "We've Been Everywhere" series where faculty, staff and students of the library could share their travel and research experiences abroad on Wednesdays followed by a reception. Highlights included a talk from our new E-town Librarian who was living in Cairo at the time of the Arab Spring, a talk by library faculty and staff about their experiences in China as part of a community training program on Chinese Culture sponsored by our Confucius Institute, and a talk from a library student about his experiences "Growing Up In Chile."